CW01372039

Introduction

Blogging is a powerful tool for helping businesses grow. It can also become a business in and of itself. Whatever goals and objectives you have for your blogging journey, these tips will set you on the path to success.

As a blogger, you should never go it alone. There are so many bloggers who have gone before you and achieve great levels of success. By following those blogs and reading up on advice like the content in this book, you can position yourself to avoid some of blogging's traditional pitfalls and get your blog noticed by your target readers.

BLOGGING FOR BUSINESS

Whether you are blogging for business to help improve SEO and attract prospective customers or clients to your website or you are blogging to create a blog as your business, blogging offers a ton of value.

Whatever your direction, embrace your passion for blogging, writing, and your subject matter. Embrace the ups and downs of the blogging journey. Run into blogging full force, and the sky is the limit!

I've compiled 8 tactics, laid out in chapters throughout, that have worked wonders for me (and the businesses I've worked for) along my blogging journey.

BLOGGING FOR BUSINESS

By applying these tactics, you'll be able to grow your readership, boost awareness of your blogging brand or business, and position your blog or business for a serious boost in revenue.

Let's get started on your blogging journey!

About the Author: Anthony Gaenzle

Anthony founded Anthony Gaenzle Marketing in 2006, a consulting business and marketing blog that provides insights, strategic advice, and actions to help small businesses and startups grow.

He is a storyteller, a strategist, and eternally a student of marketing with a proven track record. Working closely with marketing leadership teams, Anthony helps businesses uncover areas for improvement, find and fix gaps, and create and execute powerful marketing and digital strategies that generate results.

He has served in leadership roles for companies across a variety of spaces, including SaaS and Technology, Hospitality, Agencies and Consulting Businesses, Higher Education, Law Firms, Food and Beverage, and Retail.

He helps businesses develop and execute strategies that lead to significant growth in critical areas like revenue, website traffic, brand recognition, talent acquisition, and the ability to achieve and exceed organizational objectives for growth.

Applying a strong focus on SEO, content, and inbound strategy, mixed with the full scope of marketing and a background in business development, Anthony's strategic advice has led to serious growth for companies across multiple industries.

Anthony earned an MBA from Clemson University (go Tigers!) as well as a Master of Science in Marketing from the University of South Florida. Prior to that, he earned a Bachelor of Science in Mass Communication (also from USF) and an Associate of Science from Full Sail University in film and video production.

Chapter One:
Let's get started

I've had the pleasure of working with a large number of businesses across a variety of industries. Each business I work with faces unique challenges requiring unique solutions, but ultimately, they all seem to wonder the same thing.

"How can we drive more targeted traffic to our blog/website?"

It's a question that keeps many business owners, leaders, and marketing professionals awake at night.

This book will lay out 8 tested and proven methods to help you generate more targeted traffic to your website. By applying these methods, your traffic will increase, you'll be able to build your pipeline and email lists, and your business or blog revenue will grow.

These 8 methods, when used in tandem, can help you boost your blog readership, get more quality website traffic, and gain some positive momentum for your business.

The good news:

Anyone can do this. These are all easy-to-execute tips and tricks, and if done properly, you'll start seeing results in short order.

So, let's jump in!

Leading with proof

Just so we're all in this together, I want to start with a little proof that what I'm about to show you works. Using the tactics that I'm about to describe throughout this book, one SaaS healthcare technology company I worked with saw the following results in just one year.

- 81.57% increase in traffic
- 90.75% increase in pageviews
- 105.07% increase in sessions

Website traffics - Users
Blue line = 2019 users
Orange line = 2018 users

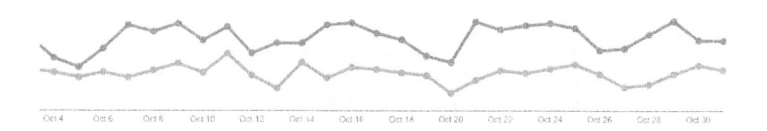

Goal Conversions - Form submissions, demo views and ebook downloads
Blue line = 2019 users
Orange line = 2018 users

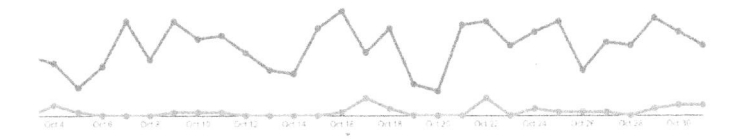

The increase in website activity resulted in a **300% increase in platform sales** directly related to the website (SEO, ad clicks, social media, and other inbound tactics).

I've seen these results repeated again and again with multiple businesses, across multiple industries. Each time, the same tactics are applied, **tailored**

to the specific business, of course, with very similar levels of success.

Now that the boring stats and graphs are out of the way (warning: more graphs and charts may appear later), let's dive into the tactics you can use to make results like the above happen.

Chapter Two:
Tactic #1 - Publish content consistently

Content should be the backbone of any marketing strategy today. The value of consistently posting new (high-quality) content on your website cannot be denied.

HubSpot (you've heard of them, right?) recently conducted a study to analyze the impact of more consistent content publishing on traffic for two purposes: Organic Traffic and Brand Awareness.

The results were telling for sure.

The study showed that sites with **4 or more weekly blog articles saw 4.5**

times more leads generated via their website than their counterparts who only published 1 (or fewer) posts per week.

I can attest to these results. When I was leading the marketing for a global content marketing agency, one of the first actions I took upon starting the role was to put together a focused editorial strategy.

We quickly went from 1 blog article every 2 weeks to 5 posts per week. To minimize the burden on any individual team member, we split the writing across the team and across departments (even our financial team got in on the action), and we also opened up posting to guest bloggers.

BLOGGING FOR BUSINESS

NOTE: You do not need a big team with different departments to make this happen. I run my own blog myself, yet I am able to publish 1 new, original piece of content each day by working with other bloggers and marketing pros.

Back to the story...

The guest bloggers for the content marketing agency came from partner companies and even our clients. We worked closely with the marketing teams for our partners and clients, so we opened up the opportunity for them to publish content on our site. In exchange, they gained a do-follow backlink and exposure to our audience.

Doing this allowed us to seriously ramp up our content production while still maintaining the high quality. Not to mention, we saw some serious increases in all the right stats. Here's some insight into the benefits we achieved from this strategy.

- 300% increase in inbound leads
- 200% increase in newsletter subscriptions
- 400% increase in website traffic
- $350,000 in new business through the website in year one
- $500,000 in new business through the website in year two

Would you be happy with the above results? I can't imagine too many businesses or blog owners would look at the bullets above and not jump at the chance to put these tactics into action.

Maintaining Quality

To make sure you get the results above, however, you need to think about quality. You can't simply produce a ton of mediocre content and hope to generate results.

Your readers and your prospects will only read, share, and engage with the content you produce if it's on target and helps them solve problems. If it doesn't accomplish those things, you'll just be spinning your wheels producing content no one cares about.

With regard to the content marketing agency case study, to ensure the quality stayed the same, each piece was proofed and edited by someone on our team. We also had a style guide in place that covered things like:

- Tone and voice
- Usage of certain terms
- Proper punctuation (to use or not use the Oxford comma, for example)
- Sentence and paragraph length
- Use of headers
- Addition of images
- Other formatting

This ensured that each piece that came through was consistent with the agency's brand. Thus, each piece was recognizable and helped with brand building.

Each piece was also crafted with a specific audience persona in mind to improve the chances that the content would connect and serve its purpose.

This quality part is critically important. While it's great to be able to produce a lot of content, producing a lot of BAD content does nothing. Actually, it does something. It kills your brand and your credibility.

Chapter Three:
Tactic #2 - Accept guest posts

If you have an unlimited budget and a team of writers on hand, you're in good shape. If you find yourself in a situation, like most marketers, where you (and maybe a handful of others) are the only one(s) available to create content for your website, this tip is for you.

As I mentioned earlier, you don't need an army of employed staff members to do this. If you've visited my website, I have a lot of exceptionally talented and super intelligent marketing and business professionals who regularly contribute to my blog. This didn't happen accidentally.

I conducted a lot of outreach to talented bloggers and marketers. As I was able to build up relationships, some of them began to create content for my site for free based on the mutually beneficial relationship we had developed.

I also created a *Write for Us* page on my site, and that has led to tons of submissions. I don't accept them all because I need to maintain a focus on the right subject matter and top-notch quality, but I am able to accept enough of the submissions that I can publish at least 1 article per day on my site, sometimes more.

I provide secure logins and bios to each author. This way, it saves me time in laying out each piece. The authors login, drop in their content, add links and images, and submit for review. Then, rather than doing all that myself, the only thing needed on my end is review and approval. In cases where the content isn't up to par, I can simply request updates.

Now that I have solid processes in place and my blog has gained significantly in recognition, the guest requests keep flowing in (for which I am very thankful!). But it wasn't always that way. It took time, effort, and building strong, reciprocal relationships to make it happen.

To help you get started in growing your list of approved guest bloggers, here are some tips.

Add Value

The key is to offer benefits to your guest bloggers. Here are just a few ways you can entice high quality writers to contribute to your blog:

- **Offer backlinks** – These should be limited to 1-2 links, and they should only link back to relevant articles on the writer's (or their company's) website to avoid spammy links.
- **Create multiple social media posts** – Let your guest bloggers know that you will share their content across your social media channels X number of times. The more followers you have and the more channels you plan to share

on, the more enticing this is. So, focus on growing your follower numbers so you can boast that guest bloggers' content will be shared with X number of followers to add value.
- **Generate thought leadership** - Each author should have a brief bio where they can present their expertise and share their social media channels and headshot to build some thought leadership into their personal brand.

Generate Interest

So, how do you get guest bloggers interested in writing for your site? Here are a few tips:

- Create a "**contributor**" or "**write for us**" page on your site.
  - This should contain info about the types of topics you present, the value to the writer, and other relevant info.
- Do some outreach on LinkedIn and Twitter.
  - I find these two channels to be exceptionally valuable in building relationships with writers.
  - Conduct searches for professionals related to your business line or blog niche. Make sure they aren't competitors, and be sure they offer high quality, authoritative views on the subject matter your site

presents, then connect with them and ask if they'd be interested in writing a post (**this is when you state the value they would receive**).

- Use your current relationships
    - No matter what line of work you're in, your company has certain relationships with partners like suppliers, distributors, contractors, and even your customers.
    - You can leverage these relationships by allowing people from these partners to publish blog content on your site (with relevant content, of course)

A few things to note to make sure your guest posts are search engine friendly and add value for your readers:

- **Links should be to relevant content only** (no spammy links and no links to product pages, etc.)
- **Ensure your authors know their stuff** (any guest contributors should be ACTUAL experts in the subject matter they write about)
- **Post content that is in line with what you would recommend** (if an author wants to write a post about why guest blogging is bad, but you don't believe that, then don't post it.)
- **Shoot for at least 1000+ words (more if you can)** (short, thin content doesn't perform. Make

sure you specify a word count of at least 1000+ words - 1500+ if you can - to ensure long-form content comes through.)

Accepting guest posts on your website helps you in so many ways. You expose your website and brand to new audiences because your guest bloggers are likely to want to share the content they create.

You boost your ability to produce more high-quality content, and you can be more consistent with posting frequency. And you are able to build relationships to help you gain more traction for your site.

Chapter Four:
Tactic #3 - Create lead magnets

As you begin to apply these tactics, you'll start to see some real increases in the traffic, and the quality of that traffic, to your website. As such, you'll want to have a mechanism in place to capture visitors' info so you can move them into your communication flow.

While you will, of course, have the traditional "Contact Us" form and maybe a newsletter sign up form set up on your site, that's not enough. This is where lead magnets come in.

A lead magnet is essentially a free item or service you give away in exchange for your site visitors providing you with their contact details. This can really help build your email lists, as people are more likely to part with their precious contact info if you give them something in return.

A few popular types of lead magnets include:

- eBooks
- White papers
- Free trials
- Checklists
- Templates
- Cheat sheets
- Scripts
- Case studies
- Calendars
- Planners
- Workbooks
- Recipes

- Product demo videos

The list goes on. You need to craft your particular offer to the needs of your audience. If you run a marketing blog, try offering a free marketing plan template. If you run a foodie blog, try giving away a free recipe.

For example, I have lead magnets setup for eBook giveaways as well as templates for content and social media calendars. Those lead magnets perform very well. You just need to figure out what your audience would want and what would entice them to give you their info.

Then, once you come up with the right giveaways, the next, perhaps most important, step is to come up with a landing page and call-to-action to ensure people clearly understand the value of the giveaway and are left with no choice but to hand over their info to get a piece of the action.

Crafty Landing Pages

Creating the lead magnets is not enough. You need to develop some crafty landing pages with messages that encourage visitors to take the action you desire.

Use minimalistic designs for your landing pages, and don't bury the call-to-action. Tell your visitor right up front what the value is that they will be receiving by downloading the content. Then make it very clear what they have to do to get it.

For example, if you are building a landing page for a marketing course aimed at an audience of marketing managers who are trying to find ways to grow the business and impress their boss, try starting with something like:

Value Line: **Rock your marketing and get your CEO's attention.**

This shows the site visitors that by signing up for your free course, enrollees can not only be better at their job and improve results, but they just might also get attention that could lead to a promotion.

Then add a brief note about what the content is, followed by a clear call-to-action (CTA). Following the above example, you could try something like:

Description line: **Download your free eBook, *5 Secrets for Marketers to Get Better Results and Boost Your Career Earnings*. In this book, you will learn:**

Then list out 3-4 bullets, short and sweet, that highlight the main takeaways from the free eBook giveaway. At the end, make sure to add a clear CTA, something like:

CTA example: **Fill out the form to access your download. >>>>**

The form, in this example, would be to the right. So, I dropped a few arrows to point the visitor's attention in the right direction.

One last note on landing pages. DO NOT, no matter how tempted you are, ask for an over-abundance of information. If you ask for too much info, you'll seriously limit your conversions. Instead, simply ask for something like First Name, Last Name, and Email Address.

You can find out more once you move the lead into your marketing funnel. The important thing is to capture their info, so you have them in the pipeline. Then move them into your communication flow and boost the relationship from there.

Chapter Five:
Tactic #4 - Harness the power of relationships

Who hasn't heard John Lennon and Paul McCartney (or Joe Cocker, if he's more your style) belt out the lyrics, "I get by with a little help from my friends"?

That line has so much power in the marketing world. Relationships can be the key to your success as a marketer, and they can have a significant impact on your ability to increase traffic to your site, and ultimately to grow your business.

To help you pinpoint the right relationships you'll need to have in place to boost your site's performance, I recommend focusing first on building connections with the following:

Industry organizations (aka associations) and events

A lot of these relationships are pay-to-play, but many can be very affordable. Start with groups like your local chamber of commerce. They often offer rates based on number of employees and company size, so if you're small (especially if you're a 1-person operation) your fees will be low.

Then, work your way up to larger organizations as your revenue grows. This increases your budget for attending events and using sponsorships, which will help with your relationships.

First things first, though, if you add enough value, these relationships can be free, no matter the organization size. So, remember to always be focused on increasing the value you add to any partner or relationship.

The benefit of connecting with industry organizations and associations like chambers of commerce, organizations whose membership is comprised of a certain group of professionals related to your line of work, and events that target your audience, is that you can leverage the networks and the authority of such groups.

These types of groups give you access to hundreds (in many instances, thousands) of people within your target market. Building these relationships can open up opportunities to get in front of more of your target audience members through content promotion, speaking engagements, and other tactics.

To make sure you're reaping the full benefits of these types of relationships, you need to offer value back the other way. Here are some tips to do that.

- Offer to contribute by joining a committee
- Write articles for association blogs
- Buy space at the next event they produce
- Advertise on association websites

- Follow associations on social media and engage consistently
- Volunteer your expertise in areas you think you can be of help
- Ask how you can help promote their mission
- Become a paying member

Anything you can do to add extra value (there's that "value" word again) for the organization will help you convince that organization to give back and pay it forward (to you).

Influencers

These don't have to be major influencers like movie stars and athletes. Those types of influencers can break your budget very quickly.

I'm talking about micro-influencers. These are the people in your industry that are respected thought leaders. They have smaller, but still significant, followings, and they are more easily accessible as compared to mega influencers.

Kick off your relationship by simply sharing their content, linking to their articles from your own articles, and finding other ways to add value for them. Don't just go in with the ask. Show them that you appreciate their content first, mention them in social media posts, and eventually they'll catch on.

This is when you can make an ask for the micro influencers you're following to share a particular piece of content or create a guest post for your site.

Once these micro influencers start sharing your content, that content connects with a whole new audience, often very engaged and trusting in what the influencer has to say. If your content is in that mix, that influencer's trust level transfers to your expertise and brand.

Not sold on the value of influencers?

Consider this stat from Twitter:

"49% of Twitter users rely on recommendations from influencers they follow on Twitter"

(Source: https://blog.twitter.com/en_us/a/2016/new-research-the-value-of-influencers-on-twitter.html)

There are over 330 million users on Twitter. So, you do the math there. And this is just one channel. Instagram, Pinterest, Facebook, LinkedIn, and other spaces are also great channels for connecting with and creating relationships with influencers.

Just assess your audience and where they are active. Look at the types of influencers they follow and who they respect. Then use this info to inform which influencers you target.

Complementary companies

Working with complementary companies to achieve mutual benefit can be highly effective. These companies are your partners, suppliers, distributors, software and service vendors, and other companies you work closely with to make your business run. They can also be companies that sell products or services that complement and enhance your own products and services.

There is often a mutual benefit without the direct competition, so convincing complementary companies to collaborate is typically easy, as long as you have a plan in place to ensure both sides' interests are met, and both earn similar value.

Once you've pinpointed the right relationships, bring your teams together to plan how you can each benefit. Set rules for the following:

- Points of contact for each side
- What channels will be used to promote one another's content
- Timing and frequency of promotion
- What specific content each side needs help getting some eyes on
- Goals and objectives (with metrics) for measuring the success of the partnership

For an example of how this works, take a look at Best Friends Animal Society, a no-kill rescue shelter located in Utah. The shelter connected with Buzzfeed (I know, huge name).

Buzzfeed has a readership of over 200 million.

Buzzfeed ran an article titled, "*We Interviewed Emma Watson While She Played with Kittens and It Was Absolutely Adorable.*" That's Emma Watson of Harry Potter fame. The article and accompanying video showed kittens who were, in fact, adoptable from the shelter, which obviously benefited Best Friends Animal Society.

I'm not saying you can grab relationships like this right from the start, but you get the idea. Start smaller and think of co-branding opportunities like this where both parties can benefit. As you grow, your opportunities like this grow and expand.

BLOGGING FOR BUSINESS

Likeminded professionals

Think about all of the marketing pros and bloggers out there in your shoes? They are tasked with driving high volumes of traffic to their company's website (or their personal blog), and they could certainly benefit from a helping hand.

Why not reach out and forge a "You scratch my back and I'll scratch yours" kind of relationship where you share their content, and in return, they share your posts as well?

Your target audience is usually very similar to the target audience of these likeminded folks out there, so collaboration such as what I'm suggesting can help get your content in front of a whole new audience who's likely looking for new insights (which you, of course, can provide).

Think of it this way. You are an aspiring thought leader in the marketing space. You have a colleague who's in the same boat, and both of you are aiming to grow readership on your blog.

Why not create a pact where you share your colleague's content, and she shares yours? Talk through the details and when and where to share, and don't overdo the sharing (if you do it will look forced).

BLOGGING FOR BUSINESS

Bloggers

I just mentioned bloggers in the paragraph above, or at least those responsible for blogs, but there is a difference.

Marketing managers, content marketers, and others can all manage blogs and editorial strategies for their companies. I'm not referring to those people here.

By bloggers, I'm referring to creative folks who decided to start a blog in their niche. Whatever that niche may be. They run the blog, choose the topics, etc., and the blog is run for the sake of being a blog. It's not a blog attached to a business website.

Here are some great examples:

- **BloggingFromParadise.com** - Ryan Biddulph travels the world and offers insights about travel, but mostly about how to be successful as a blogger. He makes very nice a living traveling the world and blogging, so this is definitely someone you want to connect with if you're in the blogging space.
- **WitAndDelight.com** - Wit & Delight is a lifestyle blog that focuses on tips to help readers live their best lives. The blog focuses on things like social media, interior design, healthy living, and other helpful topics.
- **ChaseJarvis.com** - This is a photography blog run by - you guessed it - Chase Jarvis. There

are lots of great articles about photography, but also some really engaging interviews with top people in related industries.

- **SimpleFactsOnline.com** - Blog owner Chayan Chakrabarti offers insights into digital marketing topics like SEO, technology, content marketing, social media, and so much more. He's grown a huge following insanely quickly.

While the subject matter is different, these blogs all have something in common. They have significant followings in their niche, and if you are in their niche, they could be very helpful in opening up doors to enable you to significantly increase your reach.

Reach out to these types of successful bloggers and ask how you can help them. Offer tons of value...consistently....and eventually they will see that it might make sense to start giving back and offering value to you.

Whether it's mentions on social media, backlinks, or other actions, building relationships with powerful bloggers in your niche can really benefit your brand.

Just make sure that any relationships you build are reciprocal and genuine. Don't be selfish. Genuinely seek to help, and you will be rewarded.

Chapter Six:
Tactic #5 - Leverage social media

Social media is a powerful platform for generating links and clicks back to your website. Link building by earning backlinks from other websites can be quite challenging (although also quite valuable), so having an option like social media to distribute your content is hugely important.

Let's start by looking at some social media stats courtesy of Brandwatch.

- There are over 4.4 billion people on the Internet
- 3.499 billion people are actively using social media

(Source: https://www.brandwatch.com/blog/amazing-social-media-statistics-and-facts/)

Before we move on, I want to draw your attention back to those stats. While they by no means reflect the numbers in your more niche audience, that large of a number still leaves room for a lot of those users to fall within the scope of your target audience. So, let's keep going.

How do they break down by channel, you say? Great question. Here's your answer highlighting user numbers for 10 of the hottest social media networks as of January 2021.

This study by Statista shows that these channels had the following active user numbers:

- **Facebook:** 2.74 billion
- **YouTube:** 2.29 billion
- **WhatsApp:** 2.00 billion
- **Facebook Messenger:** 1.30 billion
- **Instagram:** 1.22 billion
- **TikTok:** 689 million
- **Snapchat:** 498 million
- **Pinterest:** 442 million
- **Reddit:** 430 million
- **Twitter:** 353 million

(Source: https://www.statista.com/statistics/272014/global-social-networks-ranked-by-number-of-users/)

For starters

Now that you have a little bit of a grasp on the numbers and the opportunities out there, I want to shift the focus to some important things you should know before jumping into social media.

- Understand your audience
    - Avoid wasting time and money by narrowing down your efforts to specific channels where your target audience actually hangs out
    - You can do this by simply researching online, or you can actually ask your target audience through surveys or conversations

- Determine optimal posting times and scheduling
    - There are thousands of articles offering insight into this, but one of the best ways I find to figure out when your audience is most active is to start posting and then analyze the results
    - Look at what times and days you're seeing the most engagement on your social media posts, and then try to focus your efforts around those times
- Use the right tools and resources
    - Social media management tools like Hootsuite, Buffer, and Agorapulse are hugely valuable for making your efforts more efficient, so

determine what the best fit is for your team and your budget
    - Make sure you have the right team members in place with actual knowledge of what makes a social media strategy work
- Have a strategy in place
    - Speaking of strategy, you absolutely need to have a social media strategy in place
    - Lay out the details of your social media strategy, incorporate info about channels, specific campaigns, resources, metrics, and more to ensure you stay on track
- Measure the results

- Set goals that are reachable as well as measurable
- Make sure those goals are relevant to your specific business or blog
- Hold yourself and your team to those goals and make adjustments as necessary if you are not meeting them

Grow and drive traffic

Now, let's shift our focus again to look at ways you can grow your following and increase traffic back to your website via social media.

- Engage and join the conversation
  - One critical key to growing your audience and getting your own content shared is

engaging with others' content on their social media channels
- The more you engage, the more facetime you get for your brand and the greater the chances your content will be seen and ultimately shared
- Add comments to others' posts, share posts to your own audience, and make sure you mention the accounts of those who created the content or are connected in some way, so they receive a notice you're talking about them and they are more likely to engage
• Use trending and relevant hashtags

BLOGGING FOR BUSINESS

- - Hashtags aren't a thing on all social media channels, but on the ones where they are a thing, they can be very useful
  - Dropping a trending hashtag or two in your posts can help your content be seen by more users, just be sure that the hashtag is relevant to the subject matter you present and the brand you're trying to build (don't use off-topic hashtags just because they're trending)
- Post regularly and at the right times
  - The frequency with which you should post depends on the channel and on your audience

- Determine how many posts (this varies by channel) your audience is open to seeing from you each day
- Then determine what times you see the most engagement on your posts across each channel
- Set a schedule to post at the right frequency and during the most lucrative time periods

The key to social media success is to be consistent and stay dedicated. If you maintain a constant presence on social media and you add value for others, your following and the traffic your posts drive to your website will increase.

BLOGGING FOR BUSINESS

This will happen gradually at first and then increasingly faster as time goes along and you continue to executive your strategy.

Chapter Seven:
Tactic #6 - Have a solid SEO strategy

Before we get started with this section, I just want to set the tone. This will not be an all-encompassing SEO strategy guide. It will, however, give you a solid direction to get started on your SEO strategy and begin seeing some results in the form of a boost in search rankings for targeted keywords.

SEO is a hugely valuable activity, but it can also be significantly technical and involved. An all-encompassing guide deserves its own focus, so maybe that's another piece for another day! Stay tuned!

That said, I'm going to give you some high-powered tips for three things that every SEO strategy should contain, as well as point you toward some of the best SEO tools and resources available.

Quality content

Starting with Google's 2018 Hummingbird update, the search engine giant made it clear that they are more interested in serving up high quality content.

As a result, site owners should **focus more on providing content that answers questions and adds value for readers and less on simply ranking for keywords.**

This update drove home the importance of content that really started with Google's Panda and Penguin updates. The type of creature that kicked off the focus on quality content isn't the point, however.

The takeaway here is that you need to **create high quality content** on your website as a sort of cornerstone for your SEO strategy.

Backlinks

Your backlink profile is essentially an overview of all the pages linking to your website from other websites. It takes into account the authority of the linking pages, the anchor text from which the link is coming, the number of domains linking to your site, the variety of link sources, and other factors to create an overview of all the links pointing back to your site.

Backlinks are one of the top factors in Google's ranking factors list, and if done properly, they can help propel your site in search. To get an idea of where your backlink status stands, try using a tool like Ahrefs' free backlink checker.

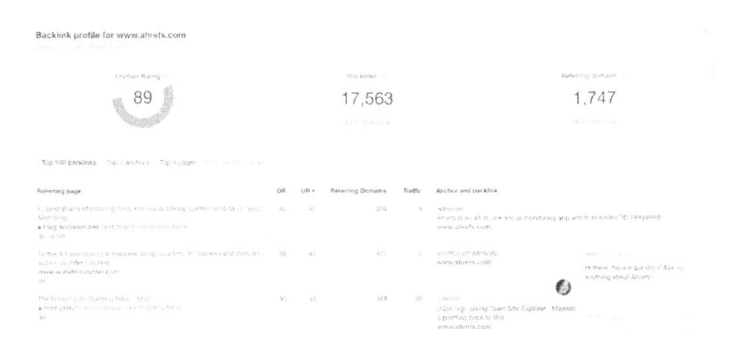

Source: Ahrefs.com/backlink-checker

The key with building a high quality backlink profile is to have links from a variety of relevant, high authority websites. Those links should have varied anchor text, and they should be natural, not forced.

NOTE: Varied anchor text means that if you are trying to rank an article about content marketing for small business, you would NOT want the anchor text containing the hyperlink back to your site to read "small business content marketing" on EVERY site it links from. Try to switch it up with variations so it looks more natural.

The best way to develop a quality backlink profile is to create great content that people want to link to, but that can take a while, so here are a few other tricks you can try (tricks that won't get you in trouble as long as the links are natural and relevant).

- **Make the ask** - Reach out to site owners with a specific page in mind and suggest that they drop in a link to an article you produced that would add value for their readers.
- **HARO** - HARO stands for Help A Reporter Out. It's a great, free resource where you can connect with writers looking for expert sources. Find inquiries from writers looking for quotes within your areas of expertise and respond.
- **Guest posts** - We just talked about guest blogging, so you can scroll back up for a more in-depth refresher. Just make sure if you take on guest blogging, you do it the right way.

- **Replace broken links** - Look for broken links on relevant websites and then look for content on your own site that could fix the problem. Then let the site owner know about the broken link and suggest they add your post to replace it.

Link building is critically important to boosting your site in search. An impressive backlink profile signals to Google that people see value in the content you share. This makes it more likely for your content to start ranking in search.

Keywords

Keywords are the terms and phrases that provide readers and search engines with information to determine what your content is about. The way SEOs (and marketers in general) approach keywords has changed significantly over the years.

You've likely heard the term "keyword stuffing" before. This is a practice that is now frowned upon where website owners would jam in as many instances of a particular keyword onto a page as they could in the hopes of manipulating search engines.

Google caught onto this practice, and now sites that stuff keywords are penalized.

Here's an example of what keyword stuffing looks like (avoid doing this at all costs).

Best Blue Jeans in Fort Worth

If you are looking for blue jeans in Fort Worth, then you are in the right place for blue jeans Forth Worth. Fort Worth has the best blue jeans hands down. So, if you need blue jeans in Fort Worth, look no further. You seriously don't have to drive any longer if you wish to buy blue jeans in Fort Worth.

This sort of trickery may have fooled the search engines back in 2012, but that's no longer the case.

Strong algorithms created by Google and other popular search engines have made sure sites that try to stuff keywords do not appear in search results.

In fact, I recall an instance back in 2013, when I had just started at the global content marketing agency I worked with. There was a competitor that stuffed keywords on their site.

They focused on keywords that looked something like "**content marketing services Greenville, SC**". You would find a 300-word page on their website, and 25% of the words (it seemed like anyway) were that term.

Initially, my competitive research showed that the agency in question kept popping up at the top of local searches. But, within less than 6 months, as Google's Penguin algorithm, which was introduced in 2012, began to really do its job, that site disappeared altogether from search. You couldn't even find it on page 10 of the results.

Moral of the story is, **avoid keyword stuffing**.

Do keywords the right way, and make sure you use natural anchor text. Vary your anchor text as well so your link profile looks more natural.

(**Suggested Reading:** Anchor text variations: Your key to link profile diversity. - Search Engine Watch - by Anthony Gaenzle)

Resources

This section on SEO has only really scratched the surface of this complex yet highly effective practice. To help you dig deeper into the world of SEO, here are some great resources for you to check out.

AnthonyGaenzle.com - As you know (since you're reading this) this is my blog, and I have lots of great guest writers, some of whom are experts in the SEO space. Just visit the site and click on the SEO menu to read articles with tips and advice to improve your SEO.

SEMrush.com - SEMrush has a great blog on SEO. They are also very engaged on social media, so check out their website and then follow them. This way, you'll always be up to date on the latest trends, tools, and tactics in the SEO world.

Moz.com - This is one of my favorites. Moz is one of the most well-respected SEO tools on the market. I rely heavily on this tool for my SEO efforts, and the blog is absolutely a must for anyone aspiring to do SEO the right way. SEO experts from all walks of the digital world offer insights and advice on this blog.

SearchEngineLand.com - Search Engine Land offers the latest news impacting the SEO community, as well as tips and advice to be more effective with SEO. If Google makes a move, you can count on this site to provide an in-depth report on what you need to know. The site is filled with breaking news and updated to keep SEOs up-to-date and on track for success.

SearchEngineWatch.com - Search Engine Watch is another great site that offers the latest news in SEO. The site also covers content marketing, social media, PPC, analytics, and other related topics. The articles are typically 1000+ words long and offer excellent, actionable insights throughout.

Backlinko.com - This site is run by Brian Dean. He provides lots of great guides and free resources to help site visitors learn how to do SEO and enable them to go execute an effective SEO strategy. Brian uses many great examples of real cases to prove the value of the insights, so the knowledge and advice is backed up by results.

Ahrefs.com - Ahrefs is a super-useful SEO software platform that also happens to have an amazing blog. The blog offers case studies, detailed tutorials, and thought leadership articles with insights you can immediately take back to the office and apply.

Check out some of the above blogs (after you finish reading this book, of course). You can find a ton of SEO knowledge and insights to help you move toward becoming an SEO pro.

So, armed with the tips above, you're ready to jump into the world of SEO. My advice to you is to start here and keep exploring. There is a world of information out there.

Just make sure to check the legitimacy of the advice you receive. Most of the info out there is good, but some of it can be misleading. So, stay alert and keep learning!

Chapter Eight:
Tactic #7 - Email marketing (build your list)

Email lists are critical to your marketing success. By collecting contact information from people who have exhibited some level of interested in your content, products, services, and whatever else you are promoting, you can send targeted emails and run campaigns to keep you and your brand top of mind.

Why is email so important?
- One-on-one, more personal communication
- Targeted messages based on segmented lists

- Keep your brand top of mind with consistent communication
- Content in your target's inbox, which they check regularly
- You own it, and you control who receives what message
- Subscribers have opted in, which means they have some interest in what you're offering

Now that you are totally sold (or at least heading in that direction) on the value of email marketing, let's dive into some ways you can get the best results from your efforts.

Segmentation

Let's focus first on the segmentation component of your email marketing. This is one of the most important parts of being successful with your email marketing, so pay close attention.

Your target audience likely isn't just one type of person with one specific interest.

Your audience is likely comprised of a variety of segments. For that reason, you should segment your email lists so you can target each one with messaging and content that resonates the most.

Studies have shown all sorts of value in segmenting your email lists. Take the following stats from Lyris, Inc., for example. According to their study, email list segmentation resulted in:

- 39% increase in open rates

- 28% lower opt-out / unsubscribe rates
- 24% increase in sales leads
- 24% greater revenue
- 21% improvement in customer retention
- 18% increase in transactions
- 15% improvement in customer acquisition

(**Source:** https://blog.hubspot.com/blog/tabid/6307/bid/32848/why-list-segmentation-matters-in-email-marketing.aspx)

Just to point out a couple of the more important stats from the list above, this particular study showed that **39% of respondents** who segmented their lists saw an **increase in open rates**. Not to mention, **24% saw an increase in sales leads**.

The value in segmenting your lists is pretty clear, so let's take a look at some of the segment types you can create.

- Interests (type of content)
- Campaign (how you collected the contact)
- Behavior (how they interact with your site)
- Funnel stage (awareness, evaluation, conversion)
- Demographics (gender, age, etc.)
- Location (you get what this one means, right?)

This allows you to send more personalized content to the right people at the right time, which leads to higher numbers of opens, clicks, conversions, and more.

Be Consistent

Now that you have your lists broken out into targeted segments, the key is to be consistent with your emails. Not everyone checks their emails on a regular basis, so it's important that you send enough emails to make sure you capture your audience's attention, without overdoing it, of course.

A recent survey by Statista showed that **38% of respondents check their email 4 or more times each day**.

That means you have a significant opportunity to get your brand message in front of your target audience if you send your emails at the right times.

I personally like to send 2-4 emails per month depending upon what's going on. This way I'm able to place new articles or offers in front of my readers on a regular basis, but I'm also not showing up every day in their inbox.

Sending daily emails, or even just more than 1 email per week, is a great way to increase your un-subscriber numbers. Just in case it's not clear, that is something you DO NOT want to do.

Allow your subscribers to determine how frequently they want to receive emails by setting up a link they can click on to change their email preferences. Make sure you provide multiple options other than simply "unsubscribe", or that's exactly what your subscribers will click on.

Give your subscribers opportunities, for example, to increase or decrease the number of emails they receive. Allow them to choose the types of emails they receive. This way you can avoid unsubscribes while also improving your stats.

Short and sweet

Have you ever received an email in your inbox that read more like a book?

These are the emails that go on and on about how great a product is, or just give you way too many details about a general topic.

Do you read these types of emails? Likely not.

I recommend keeping your emails concise. That way you get the message across, and your main point isn't missed in the middle of 5 or more unnecessary paragraphs.

If you can think of your email like a Tweet (that's a post on Twitter for those of you who are unfamiliar), you should be good.

Get to the point within 200 (low end) to 600 (high end) characters, make sure your call-to action doesn't get lost (i.e., "click this link to read more") and move on.

There are a lot of great email tips out there, so start with these and dig around. I find the Mailchimp.com blog to be a great resource for email marketing insights, but there are many others.

Here's an example email to point you in the right direction. Let's say you run a lifestyle blog that focuses on healthy living. You can send an email that looks something like this:

Hi {Name},

It's been 2 years since you first signed up for our

newsletter and we began our healthy living journey together!

We've really enjoyed having you as a part of our community, and to say, 'thank you', we wanted to send you this link to a free trial of {Insert Product Name}.

Cheers!

{Signature}

As you can see, the email is short and to the point. The CTA is clear, and it doesn't get buried in a mountain of text.

Another thing about this email is that it's personalized. That's another key. So, while we're on the subject, let's dive into personalizing your emails.

Personalization

Most quality email platforms allow you to add personalization into your messages. This can be as simple as adding some code to pull in each recipient's name. Or it can be more complex, recommending products, articles, and other content based on a particular subscriber's activities on your site.

By injecting some personalization into your messages, you're showing your readers that you are taking steps to understand them and get them content they actually want. While it may be automated and digital, it's still a step toward deeper, more meaningful connections with your target audience.

Chapter Nine:
Tactic #8 - Improve your hosting (and site speed)

I switched, relatively recently, to a new website hosting service. Before the switch, my page load time was relatively slow, and it was definitely impacting my site's performance. The load time dropped by about 5 seconds almost immediately after the switch, and my bounce rate also dropped as a result.

People were staying on my site and consuming more content. My positive stats were rising, and my negative stats were dropping. And this will most definitely be the case for you as well if you move to a speedier hosting provider.

There are lots of great hosting options out there, and I recommend doing some research before you choose which one to use for your site. It can really make a difference. A good hosting plan that speeds up your site can significantly impact your site's performance.

Take these stats from Neil Patel into account.

- 47% of consumers expect a site to load within 2 seconds
- 40% will abandon a site if it takes longer than 3 seconds to load

- A 1-second delay in page response can result in a 7% reduction in conversions

(Source: https://neilpatel.com/blog/loading-time/)

Hosting isn't the only thing that can boost your site's speed. For more info, I recommend visiting the link above on Neil's blog.

Chapter 10:
Let's recap

Now that you've finished reading (and hopefully enjoyed) this book on improving the performance of your website and boosting your traffic and revenue, you'll be prepared to do the following 8 things to generate real results:

Publish consistently

I can't stress this one enough. Content is critical to the success of any marketing strategy. Without high quality content, your website can become stagnant, the user experience suffers, traffic will lag behind, and you will have a very challenging road to achieving the goals you've set for your site. Get in the habit of publishing engaging, valuable content on a regular basis.

Build your leads

Create lead magnets aimed at collecting contact information from your visitors. This serves to build your email lists, increase your pipeline, and allow you to do some serious, targeted marketing. To do this, you need to create giveaway content like free trials, eBooks, coupon codes, templates, or other content to entice site visitors to give up their contact info in exchange for the free download.

Invite some guests

Allowing outside contributors to write guest posts for your blog can really help your website's performance. Accepting guest posts helps you add more content with less effort, it exposes your brand to new audiences, and it allows you to promote a broader array of related subject matter. There are a number of easy ways to attract guest writers to your site, and as long as you add value for them, the posts will keep on coming.

Collaborate

Working together with likeminded pros can help you expand the reach of your content. By forming mutually beneficial relationships where you and your collaborators share and engage with one another's content, you can really help amplify the impact. Work with people who share relevant, complementary content so each collaborator's audience and followers aren't confused by the content you share, and they actually get some value out of it.

Be social

Social media is a great way to drive traffic to your website, gain new followers, and enhance your thought leadership status. If you want to be successful with social media, however, you need to stay active and engaged. By staying consistent, posting on a regular basis, and interacting regularly with others, your audience will grow, and your content will reach further.

Optimize for search

Make sure you take steps to ensure your content is optimized so that it can start appearing in search. While this is a complex subject, three places you should focus on to begin with are: creating great content, building high-quality links, and optimizing for the right keywords.

Use email

Email is still a very powerful marketing tool. Make sure you put steps in place to collect contact info so you can send out segmented emails to keep people interested in your website. Segmenting your lists can help you send more targeted content to ensure the people receiving your content are actually interested, which leads to more clicks and increased engagement.

Improve your hosting

This is often overlooked. Some site owners opt for lower prices and end up with slow load times and frustrated site visitors. Do your research and pay a little more for a quality site hosting service. It will help boost the load speed of your pages, which is something Google will respect.

For more marketing insights and advice to help grow your business, visit:

www.anthonygaenzle.com

Connect with Anthony:

Twitter: AnthonyGaenzle

Facebook: AnthonyGaenzleMarketingBlog

LinkedIn: anthonygaenzle

Thank you

I truly appreciate you taking the time to purchase and read *Blogging for Business: Skyrocket Your Traffic, Grow Your Readership, and Boost Revenue*.

Blogging is a great way to create a side hustle and earn extra money, but it can also become your career if you do it the right way.

By applying the tactics presented in this book, you can position your blog for serious growth, and you can build your blogging empire.

Make sure you are passionate about your subject matter, as blogging requires time and dedication. If you love what you're writing about, you will love the blogging journey as you work toward becoming a pro blogger.

I believe fully in the power of collaboration and genuinely helping others. So, please take this book as a first step, but know that I am available via my website, email, or on social media to answer any further questions.

Thank you again, and I look forward to seeing your blogs and businesses grow!

NOTE: All work is copyright of and owned by Anthony Gaenzle Marketing, and all rights to the content within and advice presented are owned by Anthony Gaenzle.

© copyright 2021 - Anthony Gaenzle Marketing

Printed in Great Britain
by Amazon

80745303R00061